BASEBALL NIGHTS AND DDT

BASEBALL NIGHTS AND DDT

To Mary + Victories
— On your annual pilgrimge

by *Thanks for coming*

Jeanne Emmons

Jeanne Emmons
9/11/06

Pecan Grove Press   San Antonio, Texas

Cover art: "Boundary Waters," reproduced with permission of the
artist, Cathy Palmer

ISBN: 1-931247-26-9

Pecan Grove Press
Box AL
1 Camino Santa Maria
San Antonio, TX 78228

ACKNOWLEDGEMENTS

This book is a confluence of many streams, the most powerful being the presence in my life of my late father, Winfred S. Emmons, from whom I learned that words could have density and mass, and my mother, who gave me the freedom to think for myself and the courage to feel deeply. I would also like to thank Tricia Currans-Sheehan, friend and writing partner, for her steadfast support and belief in me, along with the other members of my writing group, who have patiently endured the many iterations of these poems and been midwives of their borning: Deb Freese, Stephen Coyne, Marlene VanderWeil. I am deeply grateful to Phil Hey, whose voice is always in my mind both as a poetic model and a mentor; Palmer Hall, who saw value in my poems and ushered them into the light of day; and my brothers Win Emmons and Don Emmons, who have cheered for me along the way. Finally, my deepest love and gratitude to my husband Adam and my children Eleanor and Austin. Everything I do has you in it.

Poems in this collection have been or will be published in the following journals:

"My Father Dying," *Alaska Quarterly*; "Selling the Old Piano," *The American Scholar*; "Fantasia Reissued," *Asphodel*; "Are You Washed?" "To a Friend Who Does Not Answer My Letters," "Your Underwear Showing," *Calyx, A Journal of Art and Literature By Women*; "Athena Recalls her Birth," *Confrontation*; "Baseball Nights and DDT," "Home and Heavy Air,"*Connecticut Review*; "The Possession of Susan Smith," *The Cream City Review*; "Department Store 1955 – Drinking Fountains," "Department Store 1955—Ladies' Room," *Cumberland Poetry Review*; "Academic Regalia," "Grendel's Bag," "Nominative Absolute," "Upon Looking up 'Feeble' in Your Thesaurus," *Descant*; "Vortex," *Fugue*; "Medusa," *Illuminations*; "The Terror Garden," *Kalliope*; "Vanishing Point," "The Boat," *Karamu*; "To Tobe," *The Laurel Review*; "Refinery," "Aubade," *Louisiana Literature*; "The Sound of One Hand," *National Forum*; "Degas' Little Dancer," *Phi Kappa Phi Forum*; "Metamorphosis," "My Father's Marginalia," "The Six-Billionth Child," *Prairie Winds*; "Bathsheba Bathing," *Sow's Ear Poetry Review*; "Red Letter Edition," *Wisconsin Review*.

In memory of my father
Winfred S. Emmons (1920-2000)

CONTENTS

1. Refinery

2. Cooking from Scratch

3. Possessions

4. The Sound of One Hand

1.

REFINERY

TRICK-OR-TREATING

Dry leaves scrape the sidewalk
and the night is darker than anything because
I am four and my brother with the scarf
around his head and the eyepatch is going
fast and faster, stepping on cracks, striding
ahead with his long legs and I quicken
my steps and trip over my sheet. My big brown
paper bag has no handles, so I am holding it up
by its two sides at each lit door, trying to look
up through the eyeholes at the big person
and it's getting heavier and heavier like
it's supposed to, and my brother spins
from the door and trots off to the next house,
not even waiting for anybody to say,
"and what are you?" He knows what he is.
He is on a mission of plunder, and the booty
is all the candy he can carry and I am
his specter in the sheet with the holes
for eyes, shivering in that deepening October
dark, more inside than I have ever been —
inside my head, inside that flapping sheet
I have to keep tugging at to see out the holes.
I know that if I stop he will be blocks away
before he will even notice the absence
of my round, white, skull-shaped head.

BASEBALL NIGHTS AND DDT

I can find those summer nights in the stands
by feel, the same way my fingers dug down
into the sticky mystery of Crackerjacks.
I can see my brother wind up, cock
his leg in knickers and kneesocks,
until the ball leaves his grip. I can
hear it whack the mitt, round and fat
on the catcher's hand, and then come back
smack into my brother's fingered glove,
into the oiled hollow he had a habit
of driving his fist into all day long.
When he snaps the ball again, it cracks
on the bat and there is a flurry
of running and scooping and throwing,
and afterwards a wariness on the mound,
a cleated shoe pawing the dust,
and, at first base, a waiting for opportunity.

I find a plastic ring wrapped in cellophane,
and I slide my tongue over each sweet finger,
then slip between the slats of the stands
and drop to the bare dirt, where change
can be found sometimes. The fogging
truck circles round and round the park,
spewing clouds of DDT. And still
the mosquitoes fatten and fly, so sluggish
you can slap them slow and they will leave
smears of your own or somebody else's blood
on your hand and the skin of your arm.

I do not yet know how light the ring
is going to lie on my finger, nor how
the thock of the ball into the supple palm
of somebody's glove will satisfy,
a brief convergence of sphere and hollow,
movement and stasis, how in the lift
of that leg is a gathering of power
for a pitch, long and curved, the spring
wound up to drive a whole life running down.
I cannot see how bright the fixed stars burn
beyond the corrugated tin roof of the stands,
nor the planets, either, so unwinking, so aloof
in their orbits, self-absorbed, above the fog
of baseball nights and DDT.

Are You Washed?

Are your garments spotless, are they white as snow?
Are you washed in the blood of the Lamb?

When I was five I fell into a fishpond.
It was a hot day, and I was wandering freely
without Mother, on the blazing concrete, barefoot.
It must have been the cool grass that drew me,
and the deeper cool of a spot of green.
Beneath the glassy skin of the water,
on the other side of the surface where I leaned,
the fish sailed orange like angels trailing fire.

The slime of the edge swept me in
and I lay, for a time, open-eyed,
immersed in fluency, cool and warm,
deep in the ordinary grass of the earth,
with waterspiders sliding silent
through the sunlit green.
It was glory land.

In four years I would be baptized.
We would wear white cotton gowns.
The church would go dark, and the curtain
would hiss open. The water made wavery lights
on the alcove, shaped like the seashell Venus rode on.
A clean handkerchief went over my nose,
and the preacher leaned me into clear water
and brought me up again with a loud whoosh.
The gown stuck to my flat chest,
and my hair was slicked straight back.

Afterwards, I changed, and then we sang
"Are you washed in the blood,"
and my head was still wet at the benediction.
My white patent leather shoes took me down
the front steps of the First Baptist Church,
with its Doric columns, fat and white,
like the ones you see on banks, or the Parthenon.
Perfumed ladies hugged me and gave me kisses
that left lipstick on my face. And no one knew
that, after that green baptism into the concrete,
this white one into the spirit felt as pale and colorless
as a blind fish at the bottom of a cave.

Department Store 1955 — Drinking Fountains

There were two by the elevator on every floor,
labeled white and colored, with metal plates,
one white with black letters, the other reversed
like the negative of a photograph you don't pay
any attention to. When Momma lifted me up
to the *white* fountain, I was not to rest my mouth
upon the silvery spigot with its green stains.
Germs were there, she said. So I held my lips
in the way of the bright, clean arc,
my head tilted to the side, and it was as cold
as the water in the jelly jar in the refrigerator.

Off to the side I could see the *colored* one,
where the germs had to be darker,
had to be breeding more profusely.
No one said so aloud. But while I was sucking in
the water, I was drinking in visions, afraid
as one fears things that are not spoken of.

In those days, a woman worked for us, name of Lily,
with a back straight as a folded ironing board
and skin like Mother's Duncan Phyfe table.
She wore white bobby sox and tennis shoes
and made twenty dollars for cleaning our house
five days a week from six o'clock till noon.
The palms of her hands were as pink as my skin
after a hot bath, and she slid them over the bed
to make the white sheets smooth and tight.

Negroes are just like us, Momma said,
but I knew it was not true. It had always been
the *white* fountain she held me up to.
I knew this, deep in my head, as it rested
on the sweet-smelling linen starched
and ironed under the pressure of Lily's hand.

Department Store 1955 – Ladies' Room

They had no *colored* bathrooms there in 1955,
only *white* ones, with cool, clean porcelain,
leather couches for the ladies to lie down on
when it was their time of the month,
yoke-shaped tissue-paper liners for the toilet seat,
and dimpled linen toweling to dry your hands on
after you washed with the pink granules from the dispenser.

When my great grandmother was a child in Virginia,
she had her own personal slave, I am told,
who carried her books and lunchbucket to school.
When the Yankees came, they ransacked the house
and stole the silver, and my great grandmother
hid under the bed right next to the chamber pot
that slave must have had to empty every day.
She could see their filthy boots from under the bed.

The family lost their money and she grew up
and married a poor schoolmaster, and her son
ended up a railroad clerk for the Southern Pacific.
When she went to the department store, she used
those bathrooms with a sense of entitlement,
scrubbing her pink hands with that pink grit,
rubbing off the germs from handling the money
Lord knows who had put Lord knows where.

Revival Meeting

At the piano, a man with a pouf of platinum blonde hair
played "The Savior is Waiting to Enter Your Heart"
and while we sang we wept for the patient savior
and the recalcitrant, locked heart. We wept,
my heart and I, fixed to the spot, and watched others flow
down the aisle to Jesus. Like trees uprooted in the holy wind
and fallen along the banks, they felt the rising river
of the spirit loosen them from their chairs. They floated
into the aisles, streaming to Jesus, while we wept for release,
while we prayed for the sweet insensible yielding.
People sang "I Surrender All," until the muscles
of their reason went to jelly and they melted toward
the preacher's pleading, "just let him come in,"
with that "just," like always, almost whispered, just
the consonants, just the soft sibilance, the seduction,
and it seemed my heart was just locked against the knocking,
though my body yearned to just flow to Jesus, my heart was
just bolted with thoughts that would not release me,
though softly and tenderly Jesus was calling, just waiting,
just begging. Just so easy to just give in, as if a person
didn't need a sledgehammer to shiver the hasp on the heart
from inside, because you knew, if you let reason go,
all manner of things might fly in, other than Jesus,
fanatics following you down the street with stacks of tracts,
waving their battered bibles with one hand, and at your door
whiny adenoidal boys you wanted to give a box of Kleenex to.
And also there was a stern chastity in resistance, like a hymen
that steadfastly wouldn't break somewhere deep in the mind.

REFINERY

It is the autumnal equinox, and I remember
standing at the open window back home, my room
behind me dark and grainy, that night in September
with the light off. I gazed out into the gloom
of that purplish fog, through the screen, straining
through air that was always on the point of raining,
and flames from the smokestacks lit the horizon.
The whole sky was orange that damp night,
like the glow from a midnight sun, red and rising.
The thick mist reflected and diffused the light.

God, it was beautiful, and, more, it was fuel.
It was heat and light and fire down inside
me blazing, changing me, turning all that cruel
self-doubt of the awkward, the crude child
into humming energy. And even the sulfur smell
through the window, that seemed like the fires of hell,
wasn't ever hell. It was lonely and warm
and damp. And, while I stood, a wild mood,
like a blue and orange flame inside me, formed
and half-consumed the residue of childhood.

Bolivar Peninsula

I drive there through the asphalt highways
and mosquito-clouded rice fields, edged
with the globes of low bushes, and the land
is big about me. The clouds mound up
on the horizon, deep gray behind
the gold-tipped green of the grain.

Oil pumps feed, nodding and dipping
like captive animals, and I know that tonight,
out in the Gulf, the lights of the offshore rigs
will compete with the stars, and the breakers
will bear gobbets of tar up to the sand.
I have seen them melt to black pools
in the hot sun, but at high tide the surf
will raise them up and roll them among
the broken cockles, cool them to conglomerates,
dark-hearted, shell-studded, fat as fists.
It seems sometimes as if the sea
has grown them of its own accord.

All along the road the white Brahma cattle
stand in their pastures, while snowy egrets peck
at their droppings or perch upon their backs.
Billboards bellow JESUS SAVES, and
everywhere is the urge to reclamation.
The towns have their shell shops, their real estate.
A sign outside a shack says FRESH JUNK,
and beachcombers bring their gleanings there,
rusted, sun-bleached, dry-rotted, all the cast-offs
the Gulf has refused to take back.

Out on the jetty made a hundred years ago
with rock shipped in from as far away as Boston,
the spoonbills feed, pink as oleanders.
The old men are crabbing with scraps of bait,
and in their plastic buckets is the scrabbling of blue claws.

Behind the Galveston ferry, the gulls laugh
and swoop to the fish-studded wake. I make my way
to the bow, past hot cars and sweating travelers,
to stand where the spray of the battered waves
wets my lips with salt. Time after time
I have hung there and searched the bay
for the arc of dolphins, and then, lowering my eyes,
have seen, beneath the yellow-painted rail,
a body, sleek and dark, riding the water before
the flat nose of the boat, curved like a bridge
upon which all our souls speed on to bliss.

RED LETTER EDITION

My old Bible is French Moroccan leather,
with gilt edges, the King James translation.
I could always see at a glance by the red letters
which words Jesus spoke. All the pages
in black I would ignore. At ten, I knew
God's finger hadn't burned the words with fire.
Someone had used a pen and ink, but the truth
was all in red. The rest was only inspired.

If that. By fifteen I was already hardened
against the letter of Paul to the Ephesians.
In a rounded hand, I wrangled in the margins,
defended my sex, pencilled in my reasons,
and to this day my arguments still stand
sideways beside the black letters, wedged
in that ambiguous, narrow, empty band
between the offending text and reality's edge.

In the gospel of John, the red letters made
what seemed to me, by eighteen, arrogant claims,
self-serving, insupportable. I weighed
the possibilities. Was the whole frame
of scripture then untenable? Could I dismember
belief, salvage the sound wood exhumed
from the rotting vault and add new lumber
to build new faith? Or was I utterly doomed?

Gradually it came to me that history
was like a willow in the wind, bending,
or like an endless self-revising mystery
unfurling and continually amending.
We follow it like Ariadne's thread,
unwinding through a maze. In my youth,
how could I know the flimsier it appeared,
the more it would one day have the flex of truth.

At twenty, having buried my belief,
and out of zig-zags, looking for a high,
I scissored out a rectangle from a leaf
of the thin paper. It was the blank fly
I snipped, certainly nothing from the Psalms,
or the Acts of the Apostles, or even Leviticus.
I rolled the joint and lit it without qualms.
I wanted to rise up and soar, like Icarus.
And soon the sweet smoke began to wreathe me
and the labyrinth was diminishing beneath me.

Then, paging through the red letters, I found
this: "Consider the lilies of the field."
And I considered them, low to the ground,
the clumps of green, the way the stems yield
to the least wind or dew, how the white blooms
are arrayed in glory, folded in the leaf,
green and untoiling, and I felt the stone
roll and raise up the body of my belief.
From grave dogma and corrupted duty,
emerged, unspoiled, the freshness and the beauty.

In all those years of wrestling, how could I know
that certain passages, dangerous, extravagant,
would light on me, igniting a fuse as slow
and dim as the drone of a dragged-out sacrament,
with scents upbraiding like the thin fumes
that twine from the red tip of an incense ember?
Who could predict how I would be consumed
with an urge to form words fleshy and tender
and wild as the Song of Songs? Or that the edges
of gold would be rubbed away from the old pages,
and duct tape used to mend the broken spine,
or that I would stretch a rubber band to bind
the battered leather with its carnal tatters
and gird the imperfect, human, bloodied letters?

HOME AND HEAVY AIR

Sometimes, Lord, I just want to go back
to where there's heavy air, to the town
I would have given anything to leave once,
where the odor of refineries and longleaf pines
do a slow dusky dance in the spring breeze
and a gardenia's fumes sweeten the sour air,
the heavy air of sulfur with the scorched odor
of the coffee factory, and the heavy air
of damp mud, and the must of roach
droppings under the kitchen sink.

I thought I could never love the way
the earth was flat, and everybody believed
it had to be that way, according to God,
or the way the road would just go on
and on or, over the railroad tracks,
how the ground got soggy and swampy
and tiny frogs were always jumping in the mud
and in the bayou, sometimes, moccasins gliding.

Now I think the heavy air is what I know of love,
is all I ever wanted to put my mind at ease,
and, yes, the town, even with its colonnaded houses,
termite-soft and sagging under leathery magnolias,
even with its heart abandoned, the empty chambers
of department stores, of crumbling asbestos tile,
taped-up windows, and sprayed-on graffiti,
even with its oily river and its freighters
sliding around an island full of rats,
under the mosquito-whining, heavy air.

Now I am reminded of how the clouds
mounded up on the horizon like hydrangeas,
pink and blue, edged with yellow light,
and, on the drive to the beach, how the rice fields
rippled in the stiff wind, and patches
of moving sunlight raced across the shadow.
I have missed these things, exquisite and tragic,
how they weigh on your soul and squeeze out
a sweetness thick and dark as ribbon cane syrup,
a velvet exhalation, smooth and warm as heavy air.

Air so heavy you can hardly breathe,
though you gave up cigarettes years ago,
heavy like the smell of mud and crawfish towers
after rain. Heavy like the cloud of DDT spewing
from the truck around the Little League field
in 1957. Heavy like that, like the stomp of feet
on beat two of "Precious Lord," like the
twang of a guitar string and East Texas speech
somebody tuned too high and tight, heavy like
bacon grease on greens and those fires from Mobil
glowing on the horizon, orange, ugly, gorgeous,
and the smell of that gardenia, and a night in April
gumbo-dark, lonely and warm and soft with fog
and no stars and no kiss. Sometimes, Lord,
don't you just want to go back home?

2.

Cooking From Scratch

CORRESPONDENCE
upon reading Nanny's love letters

My knowledge loads your innocence with sadness,
so the "blues" you speak of ripen dark as dewberries,
staining the page. Writing to him you'll marry,
you do not see the thorny patches of madness,
when you will gab in doorways down the street,
or curl all day, in the depression of your bed.
I unfold a letter full of plans to wed.
In it you flirt, complain of the August heat.
Years later, you will burn. Your nightgown
will catch at a gas flame one January.
For now, though, you tease the man you'll bury.
All is foretold, though you set none of it down.
Your words are dark and fluid, with yellowed spaces
in between, like a net through which the future
slips like a small fish. The young teacher
pens her hopes, but, past the knotted laces,
her death swims out, along with her children's faces.

Fantasia Reissued
San Diego, 1942

Their wedding night, they went to the movies.
Mother still had on the white linen suit
she had worn in the pastor's study. Her jacket
was buttoned up to the flounce at the neck,
because it was KOOL INSIDE the theater
even in June in San Diego.

When Mickey Mouse, the Sorcerer's Apprentice,
sloshed the buckets and danced with the mops,
his eyes had pupils for the very first time.
This gave him an air of pathos and insight,
as if he had grown and deepened somehow
into his secret self, like America.

While mother sat with her hat in her lap,
its single feather pointing straight up
as if it knew something she wasn't aware of,
the first ever astounding sound
of stereophonics seemed to surround her,
my father's arm warm on her shoulder,
his uniform buttons dimly shining.

To Igor Stravinsky's "Rite of Spring"
the dinosaurs staggered and died, and then
in "The Dance of the Hours," hippos in tutus
can-canned across the screen. My mother
rested her head against my father
and he glanced at the watch she had given him.

At intermission, they left. That night,
they lay in each other's arms and had,
so Mother insisted, no earthly idea
what they were supposed to do. My father
in all those years never contradicted
her version of how in the dark they were.

Fantasia will amazia, the promos said,
and so it unfolded in them. They waited
for things to bloom in their own time,
for the sweet rupture and the small blood
and, from bliss to promise, the purple plum
of my brother ripening slowly in the dark.

That year, someone would split the atom,
and Bald Mountain would soon be racked
with thunderbolts and deadly rain,
but they held out hope and loved each other
with pink parasols, one after the other,
opening and opening in the darkened theater.

To a Friend Who Does Not Answer My Letters

1.
Your silence is a heavy, soft thing between us.
It has had a long time to grow fat,
and we are afraid to budge it,
or even to look for each other
on the other side of it,
for who would we be after all this time?
It hurts the way the tiny pinfeathers
of a great soft pillow scratch in one's sleep,
jab one's face, and make dreams uneasy.
It is a small thing in the history of the world,
but history is made up of such small things.

2.
The tree outside my window is bent to the ground,
heavy with apples. The sunflowers, too,
have laid their faces on the damp and slowly relax,
letting go of their plump seeds. Everything bends
to earth, even the sweet fruit of our friendship,
grown dark and overripe, fallen to the grass,
food for wasps, a thing you will not bend to pick up.

3.
 Once we were goddesses in the grove behind my house,
wrapped in Mother's tablecloths and sheets,
taking pictures with the old Brownie,
which seemed to give on a world
square and comprehensible as schoolroom windows.
In it, my Daphne turned to bay laurel,
and your Diana shot me, then drew from her quiver
a single arrow of peeled catalpa switch.
Psyche squinted and snapped Athena spearing the sky.
Our world irised open and shut on those shadow selves,
and shivered into guileless rainbows arcing through the trees.

4.

We collapsed in laughter on the beds of our adolescence.
We sang "Happy Talk" and believed in the dream,
worked cryptograms out of *The Atlantic Monthly*,
choked on hot Chinese mustard, slunk into pawn shops,
ogled gunmetal and diamonds, and, later, lost ourselves
in the maze of lovers, late-night smoke, and university stacks.
Then it was as real as now, as real as my hand on this page,
more so. But it recedes into the great quiet, like radio waves
rippling through the vacuum of concentric space.

5.

We flew so high that our hearts got soft and seemed
to flatten in the heat of love. But under the waxing
and waning moon, our blood's surf kept breaking
over and over onto the real. We were awash in Kant
and commitment. Again and again we thought
to have lifted ourselves from the labyrinth,
but we were wrong. It was an unbroken thread
we followed through the dead-ends and sudden corners.
We used and were used, had fallings in and out,
had diets, sex, sickness, trips, marriage, children,
unwound the spool and took the path to now.

6.

We are not the same, but we are still standing
in the sacred grove, I swear. We are not lying
helpless under Zeus's pinions, nor have we emerged
from his head, helmeted, with owls on our shoulders.
Instead, we wait, chaste and compact, upright,
our calves bound up for hunting.
I listen for a horn or the quake of a quilled arrow,
something pointed, like words, anger or grief.
But your silence, whatever it means, is a soft thing,
abiding in the dark, not even breathing.
The past is a plume of stillness.
I do not even know if it lives anymore
or will float away on the wind.

Vanishing Point
to Diana

Each passing year there is less and less to reproach each other with.
Neither the dorm room blow-ups nor my smashing your car
on an access ramp, nor your spilling grape juice on the white
wool dress you took from my closet without asking, nor
your racing down the sidewalks of the campus, under the live
oaks, around the fountains, flailing your arms, yodeling,
leaving me ordinary, rocking in your wake.

Nor my falling in love with the boyfriend you ditched,
just when he was on the verge of Nam, nor your breaking
into the first apartment I could call mine, where I found
you eating bonbons and smoking dope with a friend
because you were pregnant by a Marxist you didn't love
who had an arsenal in his dining room, and there wasn't
anything else to do but get fat and stoned, except one thing.

Not even my refusal to ride with you to Mexico where you had
the child removed from your womb like an unbearable hangnail
and the fever you conquered with antibiotics from a doctor
with tight lips. Nor your leaving in a whirlwind for Wilmington,
your secret folded up in the inside pocket of your navy peacoat,
to marry the man you really loved, a Polish Catholic
who insisted on calling you by your last name.

Nor your driving too fast on the ice with that Chevy wagon
fire-engine red on those unfamiliar white roads the first day
of your first job teaching English to adolescents, leaving
all these hurts unconfessed, unforgiven between us.

Nor the promise we made in the seventh grade that
whoever died first would visit the other, just to prove
there was life after death, we wanted so to be sure,
nor your visiting me in a dream, leaving everything
inconclusive, fulfilling the letter but not the spirit
of the pact, nor my pointing out to you that you were dead,
nor your putting your finger softly to your lips.

Nor your widowed groom at the funeral, laughing on top
of his hurt, about how the two of you would make fun
of my letters. "God, Emmons, those letters!" he said,
prissing with this gesture I still see, so that I burned in shame
at my uppity graduate school syntax and high-flying vocabulary.

Nor your demure silence in that filmy pink angel-garment,
so un-you, that your mother picked out to bury you in,
and you couldn't do a thing to stop her even if you'd wanted to,
no more than you could put your finger to your lips when he
laughed at me or reach backwards to stop yourself from charging
headlong, naked-hearted into the snow, so the world had no
choice but to kill you, leaving these traces reaching through time,
this trail whose parallel edges never really meet, but give
the illusion of converging if you look far enough down the road.

METAMORPHOSIS
to Diana

So you come to me again,
from out of your death, my friend,
this time in words. Your face
is as clear in my mind as if we had met
this morning over coffee
and argued about something or other—
politics, God, something,
from your perspective, now moot.
But the words I use to find you are mine.
I cannot remember the sound of your voice.

I do remember your auburn hair
falling down the back of that black peacoat.
Now it lies long on your deep breast
three decades. Your smile widens
fast in my memory from smirk to grin,
and your eyes are still slitted, skeptical,
with a look of profound knowing, now.
You are as distinct as if time and change
had been sucked out of all these years
leaving you clarified in a vacuum
like that butterfly you gave me once,
trapped in a glass paperweight.

And what am I with my papery words,
but a caterpillar devouring in pass after pass
the edge of the plain green leaf of your memory,
around and around to the thread of spine,
so that after the dark spinning
and the long, gathering stillness,
the leaf may come back whole again,
as wing, an orange flame fluttering
with ciphers of spots, black, illegible?

FUBAR
to Marcellus

When you came back from Nam,
all was changed, and not just our love,
raveled from distance and deprivation,
but also the old gentleness of you,
that drifting consciousness,
sometimes drug-induced
but lovely nonetheless, and full of grace.

All I know is this: when we took that drive
up to the church overlooking the lake
and stood in the parking lot empty
of everything but us, a snake slid out
onto the concrete, with its glide undulant
and rhythmic, dragging its rattle
like the train of a bride.

I watched you take a shovel out of the trunk
and chop and chop, with your sweet lips
pulled back from your teeth,
until the poor thing was bloody bits,
nothing left to strike, nothing to twitch.
That rattle was never going to shiver again.
By then you were used to making sure
things were absolutely dead, I guess.

Contingency

Even if I had no heart,
I would find a way to love you,
moving my hand over the place
where your heart beats,
tangling my fingers in the hair
of your chest, I would feel caught by you,
gently, escapably. I would love you
with the tip of my tongue,
if I had no heart.

Even if I had no memory,
I would grasp you
with my fingers in your fingers,
I would know you and hold you,
moment by moment. The calves of my legs
would know you, and my inner thighs,
and the heels of my feet in this moment only,
sliding up your shin to the back of your knee.

Even if I had no tongue, I would talk
with my eyes answering and darkening to yours.
I would tell you stories of angels and cold creatures
under flat rocks. I would recede into
my larynx of silence for you
and I would dream voices into your ears.

And if I were blind,
I would see you with my fingers,
my tongue, my toes, my heart restored,
my mind resting in its cave of skull,
the sun having irised shut and gone all cool
and shaded where you walk
daily for pleasure and exercise.

VORTEX

We strolled the beach, a mile or so and back, under the climbing sun, the waves
curling and the dunes warming up with their gulls lifting and settling like
windblown plastic bags. Before us, in the sky, a thunderhead shaped
like an anvil, but the sun was on us and over us the blue. A funnel
in the cloud spun into relief, like something carved
in a frieze, long and thin, the paper
cone under the cotton candy,
standing out against the cloud,
another thing entirely,
behaving in strange ways,
twisted like a pastry bag,
spewing puffs of
sunlit cloud.
It moved with
the undulant look
of water going
down a drain,
compact, solid
as marble.
Breathless,
we tilted
our heads
to watch it
form, twist,
dissipate,
never
touching
down.
We
ran out of the sun, into great dollops of rain
and the broom of thunder sweeping over our sternums,
towards the beach house on its stilts, fragile as a crane,
where the children lying asleep in their beds
seemed briefly to belong to someone else.

SCRAPING PAINT

We are on our aluminum ladders
wearing gas masks with double snouts
to baffle the leaden fumes.
Our breath is loud like that of scuba divers.
And when we speak, which is seldom,
our voices come out muffled.
In the silence behind the rubber,
sweat keeps forming and condensing on our faces.

We have to keep the heat guns moving
not to ignite the wood, not to ignite
that old cellulose insulation in the walls,
and so we move them slowly, softening
and blistering layers of paint, which ruffle
onto the scraper like striped taffy,
the first white someone laid on in 1920,
and then gray, tan, and, at the last
that blue we chose to make us think
of sky and sea. Down to the bare wood.

Between two clapboards is the slit
where wasps keep coming and going
to their papery homes, and we will
have to deal with them, first with poison,
then with caulk, but for now we let them live.
We scrape and listen to the thud of eighty
years' accumulation, including our twenty,
falling on the black plastic dropcloth.
For now we breathe this filtered air, moist,
devoid of the dangerous scent of history.

SELLING THE OLD PIANO

It cost me $150 then, twenty-five years ago,
and I was a woman of some means. At midnight
in my low-rent student apartment,
I kept company with all that mahogany
polished to a hard shine. Those carved vines
luxuriating beneath the sheet music,
those shapely legs — lathed, fluted,
and scrolled — upright, staunch as Doric columns.
The chipped ivory keys had a grain like wood
to prove that they had once been alive.

The old instrument wore its history plainly —
that conical gouge, for instance, where some child
made to practice too long must have taken
an awl to it, watching the yellow shavings
spiral onto the rug. But I played willingly
and for the love of it. Singing all those *Lieder*,
laying the notes down from side to side
like a brickmason building palaces of sound.

With so many hammers I constructed
Schumann nightly. The piano bore it all,
marriage and the children napping
under a thatch of Brahms, soft-pedaled and slow,
and the first little kiosks of songs,
one-a-penny, two-a-penny, Hot Cross Buns.
The brass damper pedal shone with the rub
of Sunday shoe-soles, skinny legs stretching
to smooth the rough edges of *Fur Elise*.

My children have surpassed me now
on such high scaffoldings of Rachmaninov and Bach,
the console shakes with their scaling. They outgrow
the piano, now a century old or more.
I have sold it for $150, unappreciated.
But the ivory's patina has absorbed
a portion of my life's currency.
It is worth the same as before, I say.
It is worth the same. It rolls away from me
on a dolly down the front walk into a van,
like a stroke victim into an ambulance.
Here is the new one. Its varnished ebony
reflects my hands, stone lions couchant
on the flat steps. Where are the arpeggios
that used to rise from my windpipe like a second spine?
Memory is leaning hard on the damper.
The old strings tremble in me, faster and faster
like the invisible wings of bumblebees.

Valentine

Here's a red heart with a white doily
        pasted on with school glue.
        A heart so red you know it's beating,
        even when it's stuck away in the drawer.
        A doily so white, you think of wedding lace
        and the blossoms of the wild carrot.
        And glue oozing through the holes so that
        when you fold it in two, it sticks.
Here's a hard sugar candy that says "BE MINE"
        So hard you'll break your teeth
        unless you let it melt in the mouth
        slow, over the course of years, and
        when one's gone there's a whole box
        to reach your finger into and pull out
        another one that says "GO ON."
Here's a shiny red box with a bow,
        filled with the forbidden, dark sweets,
        so sweet you have to hide them from the children,
        so dark you have to share them slowly
        with the lights down low, or they'll melt,
        and each one has a soft center,
        coconuts, cherries, and marshmallow creme.
Here are a bunch of X's and O's.
        with their curved and straight, their cross ways,
        open mouths, crossed fingers, closed circles, jumping jacks,
        mouths waiting to be kissed, semaphores,
        lipstick prints on tissues, bird tracks, wedding rings,
        hot cross buns, and sundogs, cross my heart.

Moving in Day
to Austin

Today we leave you, lofted into adulthood,
your books a jumble stranded on your half
of the floor, and I am caught up in the undertow
and ache of the receding tide. I feel the drag
of gravity on the last grains of your childhood,
which drain now through this narrow waist
of glass and seem to be funneled far from me.
And I know this is what we have been wanting,
what all these years have been pivoting toward –
the hour hand of the clock sweeping so slowly
we hardly dreamed it would ever come to trip
this alarm mechanism, this celebratory tolling.

Even when you spoke the word "pendulum"
at three, time held sway with its inaudible chime.
And now you fly, centrifugal, away.
Because you rode off, no training wheels,
the bike wobbling from our outstretched arms,
bcause you made such music with your hands,
because you reasoned, and stood tall before us,
and we looked up to you, you came to leave us
for this high ground, your own new continent.

And I am the silver gong of the night sky,
ringing the changes, taking my toll on the sea
rocking beneath me. With an empty quiver
I stalk the stars, feel myself wax and wane
from joy to sorrow. All I had of you
whittles down to these last days — your mind
sharpened to this fine point, with your wisdom
nocked and feathered, the groove fitted to the string.
And the bow, held all that time in my embrace,
as if it were only the rocker from your cradle,
is now pulled so painfully back and back.

Oh my arrow, my prize — away with you!
No qualms. I sight down the straight shank
of your unwavering grain, without warp
or visible knots. I release you. My fingers
straighten fast, lest the string snag on my grasp.
Now, shaft and feather, you fly past my fist
on the grip, you fly true, and the wire sings
and sings at my ear: You were never mine.
Not even as you quickened in me. Not even
when I swung you in the pendulum of my arms.

COOKING FROM SCRATCH
to Ellie, at sixteen

Today, you had the notion to cook,
something Indian, involving ghee.
You made the butter slide in the pan,
and then liquefy, separate, and you
skimmed away the solids from the golden oil.

Then, as if that weren't enough,
you made cheese, thickening and souring
milk with lemon juice and straining
the curds so that they dried and tightened
into a ball inside that twisted tea towel.

The water that dripped into the bowl
tasted good, you said. It's whey,
I said, and quoted you the nursery rhyme,
but you turned away from my lessoning,
you who had, on your own, made cheese and ghee.

Oh, Miss, I would like to hold you a while
on this tuffet, hang around you, watch you
clarify, make your whey. I want to sit down
beside you, lean into your loveliness,
but even my most delicate silk is sticky
and would bind you. I have to love you from
way up here, or scare you away.

YOUR UNDERWEAR SHOWING

Red, the same red as the poppies in Oz,
it was peeking over the top of your jeans
low-riding and blue, and that lavender
crop-top of yours bared the skin of
your waist a good four inches.

How it flew out of my mouth,
like a cardinal flapping happily up,
how it flew out that your underwear
was showing and how you shrieked
back at me with your talons out
because you knew it already, you knew!
And that's why you were putting on
a belt, Mother!

                    And I felt
a slash darkening in me and brightening
to wetness, and something was going
to show that I could not reveal to you.
I could not tell if it was some innocuous
grief, like Aunt Em's, or the witch in me,
shriveled with only the ruby slippers
showing like gashes from under the house
heavy on top of me.

So I left the room and shut the door
and raged and wept because there was
a time when we had stood together
in a dressing room while you tried
on this very underwear with matching bra,
which I bought for you at Christmastime,
red as holly berries, for merriment,
and in celebration of your beauty.

FINAL

I have made him remove his seed corn cap,
out of respect, and to prevent his looking
to the bill for a crib, because he has struggled
all the term long with these books, and I think
he might be tempted. He holds the thin pen
in a hand so large it seems to want to be gloved
and opening the gate of the farrowing shed.
He bends over his essay on Virginia Woolf
while a blizzard whumps and ticks against
the double paned glass. And I am hoping
he will comprehend the dinner table candles,
the lighthouse, the rude, chaotic sea, the single mark
upon the canvas that alters everything. And
I am hoping that his car will not spin out into a ditch
on the farm road that takes him home for Christmas.

Aubade

We lie awake and do not touch.
We read. You turn away. I keep
my silence. A ceramic Buddha
lounges on the sill. We sleep.

And, over us, the heart-shaped glass
our daughter gave us hangs all night
on the window pane. Inside, a prism
waits, suspended, for the light.

Day comes too soon. I wake and squint.
My eyes open. On the wall
the colors of the spectrum hang
and seem each breath about to fall.

The Buddha contemplates the rainbows.
His serene, amused regard
shows he knows his one light pales
beside these broken, banded bars.

His one light pales and comes to nothing.
Out of nothing silence comes.
Out of silence the empty skull
in unison with nothing hums.

The sun climbs fast. The music rises.
Kiss me, while these lights are stealing
slowly down the wall beneath
the iridescent, watery ceiling.

3.

POSSESSIONS

The Terror Garden

I have made a fence around my garden
to keep out rabbits, but word drifts to me
through the screen door and chicken wire.
All those bodies in an embassy in Africa,
cruise missiles set to pierce a factory
where nerve gas might be made.

My nerves are on edge, sweat in my eye.
I bend over the weeds I have let grow
too long and feel the tug of death.
Between Tanzania and my green garden
a filament has gone slightly taut,
and, kneeling among the tares,
it is as if I were being plucked.
Everything is redolent of blood.
The iron taste is on my tongue,

Here are purple eggplants, swollen
like pregnant women legless in the rubble.
Tomatoes fallen to ground are soft
beneath their split skins and come apart,
red and wet in the hand that raises them.

I bring my harvest indoors,
and through the bright glass of the television
the world is corrected for me
by the lens-grinders of truth, the angels of commentary,
whose stock certificates are so thick
beneath their well-cut suits,
that no heartbeat is detectable.
Are we guilty only in the slick glide
of our thumbs through the seams of peapods,
the ping of the fat nuggets into the pan?

Outside, an apple falls with a thud on the lawn,
and the wasp within stirs and emerges
from his sweet gorge. Somewhere else,
ungloved fingers scrabble in the dust for grass.
But in my garden the beans dangle long and indolent,
and overripe zucchini darken and grow
to the exact length of a man's calf.

ACROPOLIS

I am only an American woman walking
in the Agora, around the broken columns,
where Socrates, putting aside all qualms
about his personal fate, went on talking
about the eternal light — where Paul came,
centuries later, and preached among
these marbles, speaking with another tongue,
though the unhearing stones were the same.
    Today a Slovenian woman was assaulted
in those woods, in the Parthenon's shadow.
She told me in English that he "lay on her,"
and she pointed down the path. We slowly walked
and found her bag on the ground, and her yellow
guidebook, and a towel the pink of oleander.

THE POSSESSION OF SUSAN SMITH

The water belonged to no-one in particular
until your car rolled too easily out of your grasp,
like those tiny toy cars you pull backwards
to tighten the spring, and then let go of.
Did you hear the water receive them
with a despondent splash? Did you watch it
embrace them softly, caress every orifice,
and lift each pocket of air to the surface
like an offering? Or did you hide your face?

For a time, it belonged only to you.
It was a hard chunk of ice you held
in your mouth, and you must have known
it was going to slowly melt into speech.
First you begged our help, keeping that green lake
at the back of your tongue like a great oval
lozenge it would gag you to swallow.
But when you confessed, the water sighed
and spilled over its banks and became
America's water. Our hearts sank into it,
down that boat ramp, strapped into car seats,
our eyes widening to the hard pour through the windows.

And then you belonged to us, our Medea.
You killed your children instead of the man who hurt you.
No man would have done what you did.
He would have killed you and the children
and then himself, and no-one would have blinked.
Not a drop of coffee would have spilled
on the morning paper, nor so much as trembled in the mug.
Your survival outraged us all.

You were the wicked stepmother to our
Hansels and Gretels. You were our evil witch.
What possessed her? we cried. And onto you
we relieved ourselves, onto you we poured
our dark, sticky, ancient secrets, our fluttering caprice,
our leaden despair, our boiling fear.

We drowned you and drowned you in our minds,
but, though you longed to, you did not die,
and thus you seemed to prove your guilt.
And our hands were clean. America was a car
heading under water, holding two babies.
They belonged to us. We had places to go
with those babies, we had things to do.
If we had been you, we would have put
those babies into preschool to get them ready
for Harvard. We would have taken them
to Disneyworld while we took in Epcott.
We would have dressed those boys in wing-tip shoes
and taken them to the symphony. We would have
left them in the car in the parking lot while we
shopped for those wing-tips. We would have
bought televisions for those babies to watch
while we got drunk on micro-brewed beers.

Our hands were clean. America owned those
babies. We bought teddy bears and toy trucks
at a brisk rate and sent them, along with flowers,
to pile up beside the water that was now
our personal real estate. We admit we
were playing Monopoly, trying to land on
Free Parking while these babies rolled into the water
like little dice. But then we did the right thing.
We turned our heads to say "OH!" and became incensed.
We threw you out of the game and divided up
everything that was yours, including your tiny iron
and your small piles of rainbow-colored money
and then we were all solvent. We each had a share in you.

Now, Susan, the invisible bonds are maturing.
Though we saw you, deep under the water, weeping for us
to help you, though we saw you pleading, slow motion,
through the glazed goggles of our televisions,
though we hardened like that concrete ramp,
though now your heart breaks again and again
over those boys, that car, over us, softly lapping
like water against the unmoving stone, we come
into our own. We grow shaggy and slick with algae.
We are not pure. We resemble again the old thing,
the deep, unstoppable thing which occupies us
moment by moment and to which we will always belong.

APPLEWHITE

upon the suicide, by poisoning, of thirty-nine members of the Heaven's Gate cult

1.

He must have wanted to overcome
the red-hot fruit of his wrongness and be pure.
He must have wanted also not to die alone.
He gazed backwards from thorny Earth
toward the paradise he was banished from,
and behold! the seraph and the burning sword
dissolved like sugar into his watery eyes.
His people saw through him as through a telescope,
a gate unhinged, exposing the beckoning night.

2.

Behind the comet the lost mother waited
(was it her breath that made that plume of blue?).
Yet the comet hung like a severed head,
its wild, hair streaming, stiff, uplifted
by a wicked wind, with its name, "Hale-Bopp,"
a name like the terrified heart skipping a beat,
a name like jiving in a rain of ice.

3.

He spoke softly and with a faith
the world has lost the knack of.
Was his belief sufficient, even if it was
his own form reflected on the mirrored
wall of the sky? Even if it was
only his own ribcage that the companion
returned to, wingbeaten with love?
His bony breast was agape and pale with dying.
Her nipples overflowed with warm milk.

4.

His words homed into the ears of his hearers,
swooping onto beaches feathered with longing.
Gulled and gelded, they lay upon their cots
like Vikings on canoes. The juice they drank
was red and sweet as the first fruit that ever was.
And, ballasted with quarters in their pockets,
fired with faith, they spread their black plastic shrouds
to the vacuous wind, and sailed for home.

5.

Now they are all translated into pixels.
Under glass, they glitter like stars. But we
clutch our remotes with both hands, the way
the faithful hold their prayerbooks to their chests.
And who can say whether the apple was poisoned?
They are as unmoved as thirty-nine Snow Whites
or thirty-nine Adams who against all odds
swallowed their way backwards into Eden.

DEGAS' LITTLE DANCER
to Marie von Goethem

He modeled you in wax and then he kept you
close by, in that dingy Paris flat he rented.
I suppose he wanted, all the while he slept,
to sense you in the room, your leg extended,
the insolent bangs, the hands locked behind.
I wonder if he reached out to caress you,
just to feel the muscled thigh his mind
had lingered over in studio. He dressed you
in real gauze, his fingers tucking the modest
tutu under the hard edge of your bodice.

After he died, they made two plaster casts,
and one of these gave rise to twenty bronzes.
Where were you when they poured that molten mass
into the womb of your negative? Have all your dances
come down to this? Did something of you last?
Or are you reduced to twenty identical stances
begotten on the fixed shape of your absence.

The wax model is now in a private collection.
Heat and handling may have dulled her features,
but X-rays show a deeper imperfection
in the armature the sculptor left beneath her —
wire, old paint brushes, whatever he could find
to keep her upright. When he smoothed her back,
he had to have felt the twisted trash inside
that only he could love, under the wax,
under his thumb — the unmalleable debris
he knew was at the core of you, Marie.

They called you "dance rat." You were reviled
by the art world as "ugly," "crude," "uneven."
But look at you now — a fourteen-year-old child
in the permanent collections of museums.
Did any part of you survive, Marie?
Did your pliable womb expand into a die
to stamp out children? Do their bones lie
in little piles now, somewhere under Paris?
The boards of the hard stages had no mercy
but did your streetwise head preserve your heart
through all those stiff rehearsals of your curtsy
before your body was translated to art?

THE SIX BILLIONTH CHILD
October 12, 1999

Somewhere on the round earth's crust
you were born today, tense, awful,
quivering with your indignation.
Tonight you will fall asleep at the tight breast
of your mother, soft and limber
in her two arms. The whole world speaks of you,
who have no name, only a place in line.
Somewhere you were born and elsewhere
another, and another, so many that we must
secretly wish death upon someone or other.

We are a ball of bees on the globe
of a hanging hive. We are a line of ants,
knotted on the drop of jelly
or blindly tunneling somewhere
with a cache of round, white eggs.
We are plural and repulsive,
termites worming through window sills
We foul our own nests and wildly multiply.
We need more death, we need more death.

The bloody thighs of your mother tremble
with the passage of all those numbers
from between her spread knees, as if you
were the end of a flat worm, six billion
segments long. Yet, though you be
limp and larval, though you be whacked
and bawling, the dry air filling the tiny bags
of your lungs, your mother grins and cries,
exhausted. Your father weeps into his rough
palms, for your hands, your feet, are perfection.
We bow our flawed heads. We pray for mercy.
You are the promise and the threat.
When we lay you down, our hopes
and fears teeter and seek equilibrium
upon the fulcrum of your little crib.

COLUMBINE HIGH

Was it that we did not want to hear
the clatter of trays on stainless steel
or see the sons and daughters of us all,
hungry for fries and something else
we had hidden from them so deep
they hardly recognized the lack of it?
Were we afraid of their high spirits,
their laughter, tattoos, deep piercings?

Oh, there was much laughter,
the tingling giggle of girls, the bark
of boys whose voices changed yesterday,
suddenly, and sometimes a snicker,
a guffaw, the cringing geek reddening,
his mind darkening with the passing
thought of his father's arsenal.

I believe we will hear the hiss of grease
our whole lives and the odor of meat,
and the scream, the shots, the bump and smell
of fear and flight. They said, "Look,"
and swept their hands from left to right,
and blood reddened the composite floor
made of everything that has led up to this.

They said, "Listen," and shots cracked
through our sleep, and they lay then,
beyond us, the guns loose in their hands,
our hands reddening, reddening, it seemed.
Yesterday our arms went around them
and today our voices, too, broke and changed.

NIOBE: AFTER COLUMBINE
Gallery 42 at the Uffizi, Florence

I watched you bend to embrace one of your daughters.
She was perhaps twelve. Weak-kneed as water,
she sank against you and slid down your body,

her head twisted to the avenging gods.
With one arm you hid her face and made
the curve of your too fertile front concave,

as if to hollow out a second womb
for her to hole up in. Your other arm
lifted up your stole to shield her from

the awful knowledge, how her brothers all,
and sisters, too, that day would come to fall.
You tried to keep her innocent. I knew all

beforehand, as I watched — how you would numb
and harden into stone, how your tears would stream
out of the rock in a wild whitewater of foam.

You must have realized this, because you aimed
your eyes at me, not at the gods. You blamed
my living womb. Your lips parted and framed

that marble emptiness, that anguished hole,
and a deeper darkness far beyond your control,
into which, one by one, your children stole.

The sculptor caught your sons and daughters, freezing
their tortured attitudes of death, of fleeing —
their fear held still for all our casual seeing.

Today our children hid their eyes and fled,
and mothers knew that something dark had bled
from our indulgent wombs and soured the nest.

The sons and daughters of us all are caught
in pixilated grief, brief as the light
on your marble cheek, hardening on toward night.

Nothing of human innocence will keep,
but knowing this does not stop our grief
from pulsing in concentric waves deep

in our core and out to the breast of the Milky Way
where nothing sucks. We weep, but every day
this blue-green world keeps turning out her babes.

The moon is sterile, but the earth is awash in tides.
From stony caverns, water breaks and slides,
and mountain springs gush from her marble eyes.

BATHSHEBA BATHING

She saw him see her from the rooftop
as she stepped into the water
with her leg penetrating the bright,
tense membrane of the surface, on which
the stump of it lay reflected, as if in that moment,
the ripple quivering from the curve of her calf
would make or unmake generations.

Her unclean blood was crusted on the hair
that curled like wires between her legs,
and, as she sank down, she could feel it
soften and drift out to color the water
of that making or unmaking. There was
a bare tinge of iron smell as she lay
watching him watch her breasts buoyed up.

And something in her gave way to him,
even then, before he called her to him.
Behind her eyes, closed now, yet aware
of his gaze on her, between her legs,
where the petals of her chaste wifehood
were even now loosening at the hip
for the soft fall and drift through history.
She knew he would call her to him. *David,*
she thought, moaning, while, already mourning,
her tongue whispered *Uriah!*

She could feel the stirrings of kings in her.
Where one would enter straight as a scepter,
there another would be struck into being,
rounded on himself like a scroll, and would uncurl
and disclose himself in blood and water mingled,
poured out on the royal sheets, the whole line
pulled from her open thighs, down to that
distant baby expressed into the unassuming straw.

To Penelope

You ought to have lost hope in twenty years
while he warred and wove around among
all those islands, blown back just as he neared

home, always backtracking, no longer young,
bedding other women. Yet you made
that death garment for his father, hung

your loom with warp threads, as if the shade
at the edge of vision could be kept from sight,
as if your flying hands could somehow stave

it off. You pulled the yarns apart at night,
insomniac, teasing out the crimped weft,
till it sagged in single strands. Your hands went right

across the loom, and then your hands went left
as if your raveling spirit could relax
in hope, as if you were not all bereft

of joy. And this way, night and day, perhaps,
selvage to selvage you embraced your fate,
the knitting or unknitting, the collapse

at morning onto that marriage bed he made,
its corner post a tree still rooted in the ground.
You lay exhausted while the deepening shade
of branches tangled, tightening all around,
and, knowing what they knew, made no sound.

TO TOBE

He walked right
through the house and out the back
and was not seen again.
                    —William Faulkner
                        "A Rose for Emily"

Maybe you saw her losing everyone but you,
all those young men turned back at the door
by the bullwhip in her father's hands, and then
his death jilting her into such loneliness,
they had to tear his body from her.

So when Homer Barron came along,
his crew foreman's arm around her waist,
his name smacking of baseball and a class
he was not born to, you could understand why
she was going to keep him, no matter what,
even if it meant folding his papery flesh,
night after night, into her white, thickening arms,
her hair lying gray along his skull.

Is that why you held your tongue all those years
of stench and dust, in and out the back door
with your market basket, ushering in those
white girls to paint rosebuds on porcelain plates?
Or was it those white-coated aldermen
and those old men with their Confederate medals,
and what they could do seemed just as bad?

Somehow you put up with it, how she could
fix those black currant eyes on you and give orders,
with the horror upstairs, and you say "Yes, Ma'am,"
and then the house be so quiet you could hear
the gold watch tick from around
the great bread pudding of her neck.
You were the only one she ever kept.

GRENDEL'S BAG

upon reading Seamus Heaney's translation of Beowulf

He would have had the whole whale-road
to work on his approach, polish his wording.
So one shouldn't be surprised to hear Beowulf,
arriving home at last to Hygelac's hall,
describe a purse patched of dragonskin
to hold the slaughtered warriors Grendel planned
to drag off to his den deep in the bog.

Odd, that in the original account,
the bard brings no such bag to light.
Odd, no mention is made in the mead-hall
when Hrothgar later hears the whole tale.
It is something one is suspicious of, like a fish story.

And yet, one must forgive the hero his,
perhaps, embroidery. It is so fitting to envision
Grendel's mother, that hag, a spawn of Cain,
stitching up the sack for her only boy.
Think of those long hours she spent rocking
in the quavery lamplight of the swamp-bottom.
One cannot help imagining her needle
catching on the scales, bending its tip
on the chips of gems the dragon would have had
crusting its hide, from long lying on its hoard.

What sky-fanning serpent, fire-fanged, leather-winged,
did she slay for that sequined skin? Or did she flay
some carrion she found – some rotting corpse
washed up on the sand or bobbing in the sea?
One thinks of the worm Wiglaf would one day kill,
with the aged Beowulf wounded unto death
at his side, the worm the griefstricken warriors
would later heave over the cliff into the breakers
beneath the pyre and the body of Beowulf burning.

All the pieces come together, one supposes,
not fused, not seamless, but sutured crazily
into a fancy fabric to hold the dismembered,
the corpus of what, in this life, we can know.

MEDUSA

Stop brandishing your sword in that annoying
way! The snakes are only a metaphor, dear,
for something or other — feminine fury, fear?
I forget what. If you want some cloying
blonde, like grey-eyed Athena, fly on home.
Look at those wings you've got attached to your feet.
You men are escaping before you even meet
a girl properly. Are you made of stone?

You think you're a hero. You're so damned affected,
with that calm show of self-control, that blithe
ego, that puffed up virtue. How typical!
You can't see a woman unless she's reflected
in that polished shield of yours. That why we writhe.
Because nothing's head-on. Nothing's reciprocal.

ATHENA RECALLS HER BIRTH

Because you ate my mother, I was never a child
in any woman's arms. Nor did any womb enfold
in warm waters my ripening. Into your deep
maw you took her, and the clench of your teeth
ground down her bones to a powder, sparing me,
whom you tested with your tongue and swallowed whole.

I always knew more than was good for me.
I recall how your throat contracted and bore me
along like a ship through the locks of your esophagus,
to the immense bitterness and howling of that belly,
and then, Oh, it is like a dream now, Father!
how I was dissolved and absorbed into the dark
currents of your veins and came to lodge in your brain
like a clot, and grew to a full-formed idea of myself.

I fought my way out of you. When you
could endure me no longer, your mind fired up
and bore down, squeezed me out from between
the great dividing lobes of your intellect,
to press against the pelvic wall of your skull.
I felt flat as the moon on the impregnable sky,
or the lady of snakes stuck on this shield I hold.

Oh, Lord, when you could hold no more of me,
I bolted from your brain like a shard of bone,
visored, virginal between my iron-girded thighs,
my owl on the wing, my spear poised to penetrate
the very dome of heaven, to take after you.

4.

THE SOUND OF ONE HAND

My Father's Marginalia

Your whole life you filled the white edges
with that pointed hand, your sharp pencil
pressing down so hard that the letters appeared
on the other side of the page, raised and reversed.
You would lock horns with every author
inside the small corral of text, and leave
these wild, restless hoofmarks in the snow.
When I take up your book, it is you I read.
And you bore down as heavily on your family
and on your friends, too, time and again,
with all your smart, incontrovertible words.

What say you, Father, to the vanishing text?
You say your limbs have no sensation, now.
Through the window, your cataract-clouded eyes
scan the barely changing pages of winter,
and all the contents of the Texas seasons.
Your tongue cannot taste, and yet your mind,
more blunt each day, still records it all,
responds with that too erasable instrument,
leaving these deep impressions on the page,
your own, and also on my page behind you,
here where I set down these words for you.

Today I walked the dog, and, though you live,
I mourned your passing. For this, too, is dying.
I see that. This slow wearing of the imprint
to the smooth plate. What have all your brains
come down to? Where are the fonts of memory?
The impress of Mother with her proud eyes
at twenty-seven? Where is the stamp
of Beowulf? Or your beloved Yeats?

Are these composed deep in you somewhere,
where no neurons fire? Are the brands
cold you press on the virgin parchment?
Is the code now uncracked, unprinted, unproofed?
I think these characters inhabit you
as a flock of blackbirds does a tree, briefly
bending the branches, until, one by one,
they lift to flap heavily into the bright,
unreadable blue of the autumnal sky.

THE BOAT
to my father

All those years ago, I watched you hammering,
with nails in your mouth, humming a tune
you made up as you went along and forgot,
the same way, now, you launch into your sentences
and stop, bewildered in the backwash, leaving no wake.

In a pot suspended from a beam in our garage,
you melted lead for the centerboard. You used
a stick to tip the pot, and a liquid with a skin
of silver rolled into the deep wooden slot.
Its medieval thickness, like boiled oil,
filled me with dread. Even the cooled metal
had a tortured softness, a dull gloss, and weighed
on my hand, heavy and bendable as a lie.

The epoxy you mixed stank like decay.
You brushed it onto the weave of fiberglass
laid over the hull, and I stood by and wondered
how those fibers could be glass and be limber
at the same time. Would they cut my hand?
With your brush you laid down paint,
blue and white, while the pipe in your teeth
sent up smoke I still smell in my dreams.

I helped you hem the sails, made of a canvas
so stiff the needle I forced through was always
slipping on the thimble I had to wear
on my middle finger, a thimble dimpled
like the chin of a child on the point of tears.
But the hurt was nothing to my pride, my awe,
for no one else's daddy built a boat.
It was like that always. Nothing was ordinary.
The cloud was always charged, alive with lightning.

You took me out on a day with no breeze.
Just once, I would have liked to feel that canvas
fill to tightness, watch that weighted centerboard
bob in its housing, steadying the boat
as it knifed through the windbeaten lake.
I waited and waited for that. I watched you
take my brothers, your students, mere acquaintances.
I did not beg, but now and then I asked you,
until the boat began to leak, until
you bailed and mended and finally gave up.
It rotted in the water. At the last
you burned it on a bed of pine boughs
in the backyard. It lay supine, like a Hindu priest,
the orange flames unfurling around the mast.

These days you are becalmed. You lean on the light,
rigid aluminum of your walker. Your legs
cannot feel. Mother pricks your finger
four times a day and gives you insulin
because your blood is too sweet. You take
a defiant leak outside the door of the garage.

And I am forever bearing you in mind.
At times my heart beats its fist against you.
And yet you are forgiven and forgiven, Father.
If I could, I would stitch you a sail again
of something weightless, something strong and bright,
to billow out and float, to take you fast
and effortlessly onto the windy waters.

ACADEMIC REGALIA
to my father

Your cap and gown weigh on me, like the vestments
of priests beset by doubt, solemn and medieval
as the Inquisition. And the folds flap
against my legs like the wings of blackbirds.
This commencement, I feel you somehow,
in the billows of its sleeves, the stiff cuff
I must turn up to shorten, the velvet stripes.

I cannot fill your gown, no more than I
could ever live up to you, with your smart words,
your wisecracks whiplashing across the rooms
I grew up in. So, with your mortarboard,
I tuckpoint your memory as if to check
the unnerving ruin of those battlements
once crenellated and snapping with flags.
I see the fissures of your intellect widening.
All that was lofty, all that edified you,
your aphasia brings down, stone by stone.

Inside the cap, a label says, helpfully,
"front of cap." If only all things
were so obliging as to provide their names.
You used to don it at a rakish angle.
I wear it flat, as if the turban-shaped
button were not attached and might roll
off the velvet square, taking with it
the brass coils of the tassel. Over the years,
your sweat on the grosgrain band has left behind
white watermarks, and under the arms
the guards have dried brittle and hard after
all those long, hot, May ceremonies.
They scratch my skin now, as I play you.

When I looked up to you, the college was all,
the field you rode out on, the way men
are driven to do, heroic against the visored
deans, the plumed regents. With your books
in your briefcase, you went at them, bravely,
pen in hand, your tenure a breastplate,
and all was noble, all was glamorous –
the glow of your pipe, your woolen herringbones.

What you knew was everything, and nothing.
Everything about words and nothing about
how to talk to a daughter who worshipped and fought you.
Everything about Chaucer and Mallory and grammar,
everything about deep structure and transformations,
and nothing about the formations of need and fear
in the red canyons of the silences you made
when milk would spill in anticipation of your anger.

How easily I slid into your skin, Daddy,
I who fought to flay you. Sometimes I thought
you batwinged, with breath of fire. Now
your bejeweled underside rolls upward,
with its bare spot beneath the wing, tender
as the crown of a newborn, and I, in the armor
you gave me, carry the words you have forgotten
under the mail, tucked into my breast
like a lady's token. Though I am the lady
and you the idled king, I raise your standard,
and in your garments I bear you again,
dashing, onto the bright field of the tournament.

FATHER ON THE PHONE, AS LEAR

And now, Father, your voice drifts (falsetto)
through the phone, wavering, after all
those opinionated years. And now

your declarations are cut adrift midsentence
and founder beneath understanding. Your brilliance
and your bite is perplexed, dulls and loosens.

Yet you are, to me, exalted, the way
the branches of a tree recover height
after the fruit is harvested or fallen.

We fought and wrangled, and we were
both right always. So now we come to this
time where right and wrong and praise and blame

do not apply. We come to the shuffling
of your feet across the living room carpet,
the lean and lift of your walker, the backward

nudge of your calves against the chair you
collapse into, this confusion on the phone.
There is no question of the man at the center

of all this slackness still being you,
like a ridgepole from which all the flapping
fabric hangs. You were unbending, yes,

hot-headed, blind, full of conceit,
but a thing to be glad of in a rainstorm,
something to hold high and not let fall.

Upon Looking up "Feeble" in Your Thesaurus
to my father, at 78

It has all the words you used to cow me with.
Now that I have the book of secret spells,
you'd think the whole of language would arrange
itself for me in manageable ranks.
(weak, infirm, enervated, impotent, powerless).
I was always getting lost in your words
and trying to fight my way back out again.
They pricked me like the brambles in the meadows
above the dunes, where we picked dewberries
those summer days, in long-sleeved shirts,
the first berries singing in the pail.

The rhythm of your hammer on the house
still rings in me over the whoosh of surf,
the seashell sound of my own thoughts in my ears.
As if just anybody could build a house,
you dove right in, enlisting your students' help,
and my younger brother's, thirteen years old,
sunburned, wanting to surf. Up on that ladder,
quivering in those long-winded days,
you stood swaybacked, with nails in your mouth
instead of words, and hummed right past them
*(Vapid, insipid, flat, dull, poor,
nerveless, spiritless, meager, flimsy, dry).*

With your thumb on the metal flange of a paintbrush,
you dragged the bristles along the planed cedar.
By August, the hair on your brown forearms
was bleached almost white, and your eyes, amused,
brilliant, were set into your tan like turquoise,
like someone's dream of the Mediterranean.
You laid down stain in just the same way
you laid down the law, or a pronouncement,
with finality, glossing the natural grain.

You packed your poems with all those words
wrenched from one context to another,
crowded, rhymed, muscled with metaphor
(prosy, prosaic, weak, puny, careless,
slovenly, loose, lax, slipshod, inexact).
You were to me all there was to condemn
and admire in a grown-up. I thought you invincible
(puerile, childish, rambling, indistinct)
and I loved and feared you to the point of adoration.

I filched your thesaurus years ago when I
got serious about words, but I think of it still
as your book, its broken spine repaired
with duct tape, and the pages brittle,
edged with yellow. In our stretch of the Gulf,
the offshore rigs darkened the water, and left
globs of tar on the sand *(bald, colorless,*
watery, tame, languid). As I write this,
the words are draining out like floodwaters
from the locks of your mind. *(hazy, dim, nebulous,*
misty, uncertain, blurred, faint, vague).

All your language pours through me now.
Sometimes it rolls in like a rough surf,
washing up onto the lumps of melted tar,
which cool and roll into balls, picking up bits
of shells and sand, lumpy conglomerates,
seeming to catch the drift of everything.
And sometimes the words lie perfectly still,
with all their allusions settling down to clarity,
as clean as the waters of a chlorinated pool.

MY FATHER DYING

Your eyes looked past me, through me, windows on a sky
I could not reach, all your fire and featheredge come down
to a profound gentleness, your smile a giving way to gravity.
The forehead I kissed was stretched thin on your skull,
shiny as the skin of scalded milk cooling in the pan.

It seemed that before my eyes your body evaporated
toward weightlessness, diminishing to the translucence
one's breath has on a cold day. Oh, Daddy, you were lovely,
an ethereal thing, a wisp of mist curling on the rice fields,
something the wind dissipates or the sun burns off by noon.

And then I turned my back. And when I saw you next
you were cold and solid as that statue Michelangelo
could picture all along, they say, beneath that hunk
of Carrara marble gouged from the quarry — perfect,
patient under the slow ring of the releasing chisel.

Flying South to My Father's Funeral

Once you were bodiless, I could conjure you
on take-off, grasping your immaterial hand.
I tried to talk to you, but the words were frozen,
as when I was a child and you were God.

We climbed and I felt the weight of my own body
pressing me back, the shawl of gravity dragging.
I leaned my head against the cold window,
and things diminished below. The cars on the highways

shrank and slowed to a crawl. The whole earth
flattened to formal fields and unassuming
tones of brown. Inside the fallow grid
of roads and plots, the Minnesota lakes

were wells of grief. They stiffened, round and rough,
as if the wind had whipped them into whitecaps
before they froze, ringed by the turbulence
of birchtree banks. They passed below us,

ceremonially, like boats. And the curve of the river
crossed boundaries, pushing through the plats
beneath its floes, a pressure in the skull
urging release, something lodged in the throat.

I dozed and woke and dozed and woke again
to the flow of bayous bending between the soft
shores of cypress. Look, Daddy! I swear I saw
a green haze on the rice fields, suspended.

Then the ear-popping drop, the pressure shifting,
the weightlessness, the steep bank, the leaning
on the warm window pane, the clutch and fisting
of my heart, Father, on your absent hand.

The shadow of a small bird swiftly expanded.
Was it a hawk or an eagle arrowing in?
The beak, enormous, pointed, slid on the ground
and fastened to the wheel as we touched down

Father's Day

It is not even half a year since you died,
and I want, as I have wanted every year,
to tell the truth about you, to you and to myself,
to exaggerate neither the bitter not the sweet.

How many hours of my life have I spent
standing at wire racks and tiers of cards
that bear no trace of you, remote in your books,
with your pipe in your teeth and your pencil sharpened?

No hint of the heart-stopping barks at dinnertime,
or kisses lingering on Mother's mouth,
or that smug, bemused look, that quick, hard hug
and whimpered "hmmp" when you were pleased with me.

Each year I would choose a blank card
upon which I would compose you, Daddy,
in a kind of truth, as you almost were, in my eyes,
mingling my own ideals with yours, omitting faults.

And these I would present to you, My Father Seen
in a Certain Light, and you loved these, you loved
the construction I put on you, knowing how we walked
together that fine line between reality and dream.

And toward the end it was a dying light I saw you in,
by which the threads of your image shone rose and gold
and seemed to knit up over the flaws and threadbare patches,
and this I faithfully laid down in those last cards.

And there would result an image of you, rendered
in all honesty not quite accurately, a small re-weaving
of the brightest fibers in your rough-spun coat.
But, even so, all those shallow tiers of canned sentiment,

all those flimsy carousels of nostalgia, flung my heart
wildly about and left me with a semblance of envy,
and I would come sometimes to tears, finding
no common words to approximate our troubled love,
our honor, pain and pride, and now, this grief.

THE SOUND OF ONE HAND
to my father

The yellow Buddha I stole from you
sits in Lotus position and grins broadly,
fans himself, and is a cigarette lighter.
Is the fan to make the flame go higher?
Or to blow the smoke away, figuratively,
when a person leans down for a light?
No one leans down. I have never known
there to be any flint or fluid in him.
You smoked a pipe and never used
anything but wooden Diamond matches,
which you struck on the sole of your shoe.

So the Buddha was always reduced to himself,
a fixture in your book-heavy study,
a metaphor divested of his uses.
He was a gift from a student of yours who thought
you more exotic than you were, I guess,
who did not know you regularly attended
the Baptist church, singing "Just as I Am"
week after week at Wednesday prayer meeting.
The student only knew that you could sure
talk about Pound and Ginsberg and therefore
would surely want a lighter like a Buddha.
And maybe he was right, because you kept it
all those years in plain sight on your desk.

I have appropriated it for my own study
which has yellow walls the exact color
of his skin. I do not look for a light.
I gave up smoking long ago. Still,
something in the pendulous earlobes,
the bald head, the bulbous belly, draws me.
I like the way he just goes on grinning
and holding the fan, for which he has no use.

I do not require of him the brief flame,
the burning. But I find myself dreaming
of a long drag, a quickening ember, and
the growing suspense of an ash before falling.
Whenever I see him, I think deeply of you, Father,
and grow still, listening for the sound of one hand.

More about Jeanne Emmons' *Baseball Nights and DDT:*

"I must remember everything," Pablo Neruda wrote, and Jeanne Emmons exhibits that same urgency and appetite, intent on capturing the losses of a Southern childhood, friends dead or drifted away, children moving on. These poems, written for keeps and employed like wedges for opening the poet to vital sources, frequently ask questions, and the frequency signals an unquenchable desire to know and experience. Crucially, in her quest, she demonstrates the wisdom of Pound's imperative that words should "cling close to things," for hers perform the magic of invoking whole, living worlds, including even those of American madness (Columbine, Susan Smith). Culminating the book is a long elegiac father-daughter sequence that rivetingly recapitulates and develops a chord struck by the book's first poem, which recalls Halloween ghosts hurrying to gather treats. Like Pater "expanding the interval" of our brief lives, Emmons, in the face of mortality, refuses not only to blink but also to despair—she's a shipwreck survivor singing in the lifeboat. As if echoing the Victorian's "hard, gemlike flame," Emmons writes in "Refinery" of "a blue and orange flame inside me," and the readers of this book will feel that heat and be grateful for it. **—Philip Dacey**

As a sculptor rescues the essential from a weight of stone, Jeanne Emmons rescues childhood's freshness from pesticides, oil pollution, and religious strictness, rescues a vivid past from the slough of memory, rescues family love from the tangle of family oppositions.

Her ability with both poetic forms and free verse is impressive. Her language has a sculpted quality, a range of texture from the tough and tensile to the delicate and subtle. The result is a gallery of the essential, opening out from one specific life to the historical and mythical lives we all share.

The final section, exploring a daughter-father relationship, neither whines nor accuses nor sentimentalizes, but struggles through to an emotional honesty as moving as it is rare in today's poetry. Both the daughter and the father are people it would be an honor to know. **—James Doyle**

Jeanne Emmons is a poet of tremendous range – from growing up in the oil fields of east Texas to wonderful doubts and affirmations about Jesus, from loving poems about her children to exquisite retellings of classical myths, and the best series of poems about a father that I have ever read. She shows intelligence and craft in every poem and grace in every line – with a finely tuned musical sensibility that will gain the admiration (if not outright envy) of all writers who read her. These are poems not only to read, but to live with a long time.

—Phil Hey

Jeanne Emmons' *Baseball Nights and DDT* explores themes of memory—its cycles of loss and letting go, as well as its cycles of reclamation and rediscovery—with a rigor and generosity that is ultimately regenerative and redemptive. These poems consistently reveal a steadfast yet sympathetic eye, a sensibility that is both exacting and deeply compassionate, and a use of language that possesses both a razor-sharp clarity and voluptuous lushness. Her deftly-executed and compelling narratives resonate and linger in the reader's mind with their empathetic voice, subtle humor, finely-wrought language, and gorgeous imagery. *Baseball Nights and DDT* is a marvelous and moving collection of poems.

—Lee Ann Roripaugh

Byers, Cluster R. *Revisions of Visions.* 2005.
    ISBN: 1-877603-81-3 $12
Byrne, Edward. *Tidal Air.* 2002.
    ISBN: 1-931247-00-5 $12
Cervantes, James. *Live Music.* 2002.
    ISBN: 1-931247-02-1 $7
Challendar, Craig. *Dancing on Water.* 2005.
    ISBN: 1-931247-20-x $12
Cruz, Eric. *Through the Window.* 2002.
    ISBN: 1-931247-08-0
Fargnoli, Patricia. *Small Songs of Pain.* 2004.
    ISBN: 1-931247-17-x $10
Gilgun, John. *In the Zone: the Moby Dick Poems.* 2002
    ISBN: 1-931247-13-7 $7
Haddad, Marian. *Somewhere Between Mexico and a River Called Home.*
    2004. ISBN: 1-931247-18-8 $15
Hall, H. Palmer. *Reflections on Writing, Publishing & Other
    Things.* 2003. ISBN: 1-931247-03-x $7
Hamby, Jerry. *Lines Drawn in Water.* 2003.
    ISBN: 1-931247-16-1 $10
Hughes, Glenn. Sleeping at the Open Window. 2005.
    ISBN: 1-931247-25-0 $8
Lyons, Bonnie. *In Other Words.* 2003.
    ISBN: 1-931247- 15-3 $12
Kasper, Catherine. A Gradual Disappearance of Insects. 2005.
    ISBN: 1-931247-22-6 $8
Kirkpatrick, Kathryn. *Beyond Reason.* 2004.
    ISBN: 1-931247-09-9 $12
McCann, Janet. Emily's Dress. 2004
    ISBN: 1-931247-21-8 $8
Mohring, Ron. *Beneficence.* 2003.
    ISBN:1-931247-11-0 $7
Pedraza, Venetia June. *Porcelain Dolls Break.* 2004.
    ISBN: 1-931247-19-6 $7
Stryker, Rod C. *Exploits of a Sun Poet.* 2003.
    ISBN: 1-931247-12-9 $12
Stryk, Dan. *Taping Images to Walls.* 2002.
    ISBN: 1-931247-04-8 $11
Thomas, Larry. *The Woodlanders,* 2002.
    ISBN: 1-931247-05-6 $7
Trounstine, Jean. *Almost Home Free.* 2003.
    ISBN: 1-931247-14-5 $15
Valdata, Patricia. *Looking for Bivalve.* 2002.
    ISBN: 1-931247-07-2 $7
Wendt, Ingrid. *Blow the Candle Out..* 2002.
    ISBN: 1-931247-06-4 $7